BECAUSE TIME

poems by

Liz Abrams-Morley

Finishing Line Press
Georgetown, Kentucky

BECAUSE TIME

.

ACKNOWLEDGMENTS

The author thanks the editors of these journals and anthologies where some
of these poems appeared in these or earlier versions:

Solstice Literary Magazine (Contest finalist, 2023):"Your Sister, Wyeth,
     Shoes"
Philadelphia Stories: "Her Too; Ledor Vador"
Connecticut River Review: "Olivia and I Learn About the Nature of Time and
     Space"
Passager: "Write Your Hope for the New Year"
Persimmon Tree: "Postcards from Epiphany, 2021"
Passager: "My Father, 13 Years Gone;" "On June 6, 1968;" "That Day" (These
     published poems were part of the prize-winning folio for Passager Poet of
     2020.)
The Write Launch: "Growing Up Townie"
Where I Want to Live: Poems for Fair & Affordable Housing: "Her Stake"

Publisher: Leah Huete de Maines
Editor: Christen Kincaid
Cover Art: Detail from "Next Step" © Pam Abrams-Warnick
Author Photo: Judy Gelles
Cover Design: Elizabeth Maines McCleavy

Order online: www.finishinglinepress.com
also available on amazon.com

Author inquiries and mail orders:
Finishing Line Press
PO Box 1626
Georgetown, Kentucky 40324
USA

Contents

From Jewish Lexicon:
L'dor va'dor PRONUNCIATIONS l'dor vador   (leh-DOR vah-DOR)
• adv. From generation to generation.
• "A major component of Judaism is passing traditions l'dor vador to
keep them alive."
• לדור ודור ledor vador - 'for all generations, forever'

These are for the next generation,
Rebecca and Sarah, Calvin and Wesley

PROLOGUE

REVISIONIST GRIMM

This day a child walked
Down a breadcrumb path on soft
Paws and entered the

House of a dragon
She was cold but knew fire heats
It was dark but she

Knew fire illumines
So she taunted the dragon
Until he roared then held

Her hands to the flame he made
Until they became flannel
Then she wiped from his face

Salty green dragon tears
Which puddled in cleft rock
To the depth of a small sea

YOUR SISTER, WYETH, SHOES

This morning you're thinking about shoes,
of a painting your sister is trying to complete,
socked feet of all those young men, her son's
friends come to make a shiva call, to visit
a mother in shock, grieving, boys removing
sneakers so as to not soil her carpet.

Fifteen years later, she paints what she still sees,
that shoe pile by the door. When you
watch her, you are mind-walked around

other pedestrian testaments:
D.C., the Holocaust Museum—
everyone notices the shoe room, your guide
says while you try to erase imprinted images: scuffed
baby shoes, ragged laces on brown work boots
your mother would have said *had plenty of life
in them still.* Children killed by gun violence

are represented by so many colorful tee shirts over crosses
in front of one old city church, and these rustle,
ghostly moans in slight breeze, but shoes, one pair
for each lost civilian Iraqi set in twos across the grassy
public mall in front of Independence Hall look,
from a slight distance almost playful,

as if the dead had lined up in a game of Simon Says
and Simon said rise skyward, or maybe they
were lifted by the pull of a UFO, or perhaps
raptured, in any case, called home to a place
of bare feet only. Something so present in
the absence of the human form,

as you knew Wyeth knew. When you saw
his studies for a painting titled *The Fisherman,*
you saw a study in erasure: sketch after sketch of less and
less

of the man until, in the final oil—a room, fishing boots by
the slightly ajar door. Or maybe not ajar. The room
you've mostly forgotten.

The dead you can't kick off like old shoes
slip through cracks, step lightly across
the worn floorboards.

THAT DAY

Nightmares are what birthday parties
are made of, or so you quipped, hustling
through your children's childhood years,
a distracted draftee, checking boxes on
mental forms. You didn't know you
wrote your own job description.

Now cherry blossoms fill your window,
a tree grown, once again, too tall
despite careful trimming, the flowers
a blessing of pink promise while
pandemic spring slogs through weeks
long as months and months

long as dog-years, though lucky dogs
still touch noses and wrestle in
Washington Square while we, mouths
masked, can only smile with our eyes
and wave from safe distances.
Grandbabies are seen only

on screens and seem sweet enough
to be a taste on a dry tongue,
a hunger of arms. *Regret is*
stupid, your son, only eight years old
and so wise, once lisped. You
remember that day:

the slow hike through woods, your gaze
on his unmarked, gentle face,
how completely you listened.

BECAUSE TIME IS A MIND-FUCK, I TELL HIM

kitten perched at the top of my new bookcase looking for trouble, no judgment so he dive-bombs down so now I am time traveling this morning. This is what time travel is: one split second and I'm thirty rather than seventy, my two-year-old daughter down the hall in a house we haven't lived in for more than a decade, the student-cheap bookcase of cinderblock and board lines one full wall of the room she's in, and I am on the phone a hallway away. Phones are still attached to walls by squiggly wires when I hear "Mommy Mommy look!" right after the crashing of a dozen heavy books. Now I crash down the hall, phone dropped—see her proud face beaming from the third shelf up where she crouches in the little mint green pantsuit I found the week before at the hospital thrift shop. She's already been to the hospital ER at least twice with cuts and bumps but she's laughing. Fearless.

And time travel is this; I am standing at the edge of the Atlantic in Wellfleet beside a mother of young children, my grandchildren just departed from their visit, and for a moment I am the young mother and I watch the children dip green buckets into the water as the waves roll over their bare toes and then they are my bare toes, it is my bucket and I am the child who grew up by the Atlantic. Not memory, this, more dislocation, relocation, all of these moments for the duration of three waves crashing and ebbing, coexisting in me on that beach.

This is why I always bring home the ashes after each loss, half a dozen small, carved wood boxes now in the corner cabinet I remember from a corner of my parents' first house. This is why I opt to keep the ashes, I tell my husband, because I need the reminders that this kitten is not the last cat although some days they are the experience of all cats, aren't they? The older I get the more time circles the way each cat at some point circles himself three, four, five times before settling onto my lap curled up like a cinnamon roll. This is why I make poems, make collages, I tell him—that need to leave evidence that I was here for some moments in this body, particular.

GROWING UP TOWNIE

i. Spring

In a few days I'll be a few days
closer to the grave, vintage, I'm
a Smith Corona, sticking keys

on J or L, clack-tapping like
kitten heels on concrete paths we
paced outside the ivied walls,

no diamonds in the rough, not even
cubic zirconium, no, just the paste
stones on rings we flashed as if

these signified engagement in a world
we could not comprehend let alone
enter, oak doors, lead mullioned windows,

rooms dark, tomblike, smelling of cherry
pipe, young men wearing the brocaded
yoke of entitlement. In May

there was too, an almost cloying
perfume of magnolia which clung
to our hungers, to our gauzy skirts.

We stood outside, mannequins, until
a few of us sawed our ways out of display
cases good girls were nailed into. We

climbed the loft stairs that led to safe
silence over your parents garage,
carried mason jars of purloined vodka.

Somehow we never tumbled
down to where our parents sat and wove
theories about how they surely knew

what they surely didn't know. So long
ago; the past is a vast and shifting landscape,
a nice place to visit

as long as you don't try to make
claim, stay, plant a flag
and insist on living there.

ii. Summer at the Shore

I count backwards, scratch
subtraction problems into
margins of thought as I roll
under, try to recall the sound
of my mother.

How the surf tossed us at least
once each summer, head over
heels, agitated as if
in the heavy soil cycle and we
could not open our eyes

against the saline sting.
It's hard sometimes to swirl
in the dark, not knowing
which way is down—you can't
release your tucked knees, can't

bring your feet to—not exactly
solid ground—the shifting sand
bottom pitting constantly but
at least a something and finally
you come face to sky, air.

iii. Autumn: City

Saturday: a burst of bloom and eighty degrees. On Monday, your friend Sarah says *it felt like such a great lesson in impermanence, Sunday, gray, the cold storm.* Think of the magnolia petals, how, in your home town, they opened like fireworks and scattered on the rain slicked pavement as if in one fluid movement every spring. *Life's like that*, Sarah says, the chill closing back in over the grit-city neighborhood where you are home.

MY FATHER, 13 YEARS GONE

Speaks to me from the stoop I've not left in weeks, magnolia blossoms raining down on my drive, week five or six—we've all lost track of the days— and he's pulled by scent and he says as he draws in a loud inhale, *almost Mother's Day again and all those magnolias, the sunlight, how I lined you up under magnolias, enough shade to gray-scale the black and white prints I made for your mother every year. I only wanted to picture you in sunlight and you were the one, always, squinting into the future, a little stood back, some shadow bisecting your cheek forcing me to reposition the camera over and over, May after May. You sought out shadows like some soul crawled out from the clouds that hovered over my childhood—pestilence, war, famine—every plague but the frogs and I wanted my daughters bathed in sunshine, for them to grow sturdy as the trunks of old magnolias.* Silence, then as one by one the petals fall on me, another loud breath and *I was five when the Spanish flu took a sibling or two from me, when the world hid behind masks and stayed out of sunlight. There is life after so much death, I tell you, but it ain't easy kiddo*, he's saying in that way he's always said it, gruff, kind, then *you can do it.* I'm squinting hard and my arms reach for him but I'm just swimming in air, just batting dust motes lit and golden now, motes of nothing, bright and slanting upward, upward.

ON JUNE 6, 1968

My father reminisced about *that Tuesday*
twenty-four years before, when his buddies
disgorged and Normandy's shores bloomed red
Like a bucket of poppies, he said,
flowering wherever teenaged boys bled out,

on sand or in water, salt bathing and burning wounds
the way my father taught us to cure blisters and cuts
all those summers by the sea. *Just wade*, he'd say,
that'll clean it out. I was GI age that night in L.A.

Bobby K. gave the last speech he'd ever give,
some of my generation fighting
in remote jungles, wading into leech-
infested swamp water, a war so much
less clean or cleansing than my father's

war, Bobby on the floor of the kitchen,
Ambassador Hotel, as June 5 bled into
the wee hours of June 6, 1968. *That Thursday*,
he was dead and for we who were coming of age
watching assassinations pile one on the other—

King before RFK, JFK five years before— the world
itself was writhing, its wounds too jagged to be healed
by sea water. Still, I mostly remember now how I sat,
June 6, 1968 becoming June 7 then 8, swaddled
in white bandages, feet elevated, heat itching stitches

pulling tight sides of a wide, surgical slice
across me, hip bone to hip bone, my ovary,
ready to explode and spew poison having been
ripped out, *just in time.* Lost in the clot of *much more
critical losses*, my own small wound bled until

it stopped bleeding, my crimson scar,
at first so angry, paling to shell pink
and all but forgotten in those
tumultuous decades after.

METAPHOR

The storm gets violent and we can't keep it
Out of the living room. The roof still leaks.

A grand turduckan of disasters raging—
Wildfires west, tornadoes east, everywhere

Pandemic stats the first thing we read
Each morning. Long ago, recess over,

The young boy, tears streaming down his face,
Made the perfect metaphor and said

No, I ain't crying, Ms. A.M.
The sun just made my eyes all out of breath.

In the same class, another child said
The rain came down like a cemetery,

By which he meant not loss, but hushed peace.
How you say the world, I learned,

Is how you see it. Now in the summer of
Spotted lanternflies everywhere, see their

Useless beauty, their beautiful destruction. My sister
Sends photos of skies over San Francisco Bay.

They look like a Mars Scape, I write. *It never gets*
Dark here, she says. In my dreams I am rescuing

Everyone but no one stays rescued, one side of our
Country on fire, the other literally underwater.

What's the death toll? You ask until
Numbers become abstraction and

Something about masking feels like metaphor,
Like simile, though nothing follows *as* or *like,*

And though we've come to believe *unprecedented*
May be the most overused word in the English language,

Face it: there's nothing quite
Like any of this anymore.

POSTCARDS FROM EPIPHANY, 2021

i.

My soles are worn thin, boots once new—
Women's March, 2017, D.C., Day 2 of this
nightmare that refuses to end.

These broken-down boots. Every Tuesday
on the corner, cold wind, cold toes, January 5, 2021:
the sign John hands me reads *Surrender Donnie*

and we laugh. The usual bus driver beeps, passersby
give thumbs up here in Philadelphia where bad things
are alleged to happen, where good things are happening.

ii.

Every Wednesday in this Covid year, second graders and I are
glued to screens, zoom being education now. January 6: Flee
the freeze, snooze through, we discuss how animals prepare
for and deal with winter—next week, adaption. Today we stay
with hibernation, a video of grizzlies tearing a beached whale
sinew from sinew, filling bellies with blubber and meat before
each will head into a burrow and sleep until spring. Fiona
says she'd eat lots of pasta. Marquis shuts his eyes against
the brutality as sharp, white, bear teeth and claws tear flesh.
Snouts are buried into flanks of a once magnificent beast.
I'm buoyant today, filled with hope because in Georgia, the
reverend filling MLK's shoes in the pulpit will be seated in the
Senate, and only a thin ligament stretches between win or lose
for the last seat and control of the body.

As soon as the kids sign off, I switch to election news, instead
of statistics see white angry faces, rampaging, dismantling,
outside, inside—*sanctuary of democracy,* a reporter yells
above sounds of tearing, ripping, destroying.

iii.

The whale, the bears, the blood on white incisors, the guttural growls.
The shrieks of torn things. I am not making metaphors.

iv.

A duly elected congresswoman, workplace under siege, calls a reporter,
she says, *from a sort of secure location.* She says *I'm a mother* (ragged
breath) *last night I told my husband where to find my will.* She says *I
was in a more secure location but some of my colleagues from the other
side refused to mask so I asked to be moved here—it's not as safe.* Her
voice shakes. Deadly virus or deadly mob; she is sailing between Scylla
and Charybdis.

v.

Night rolls to the next day without sleep.
January 7: roll out a yoga mat, grateful for zoom.
Ten of us, mothers, sisters, Americans log on
seeking an hour when someone else
will remind us to breathe.

Hang on little tomato I say
to my own heart.

ON CHILD TIME

Listen, I told her, *for the sounds*
You cannot hear: Chlorophyl rising
Up-stem to leaf, the bird inside

A sky-blue egg, sleeping, not yet
Quick or feathered. Listen for it:
The crackle of sunbeam through

Cloudless air. A seed, under warm
Earth, unfurls and breaks. Can you
Make out the sizzling split of its shell?

NATURAL MOTHER

Heat rising as if July elbowed
May and June aside, sweating
Azaleas into a forced-march
Bloom before wither. How

Did you get here, you wonder,
Beyond this house, this sun-
Scorched earth warming, white
Bears losing their ice too fast, too soon.

Habitat, the children repeat, a word
They define as place, as weather:
Rain forest, baked desert, sea. You
Bring them a film of her:

Octopus become teacher become
Film star from a kelp forest. You
Show the kids her undulating home but instead
They want to know: *Could this octopus grow*

Her head back and not just regenerate an arm?
So you recall sea stars, stumps of new limbs, how these
Mesmerized you when you were their age
And after you leave them, you find yourself yearning

For that lost story: the whale mother, how she
Carried her dead baby on her back, how she
Swam her grief on her back for days until she
Could let it go. Last night, in your city,

Another child killed, another *wrong place, wrong
Time*, another *just reaching for a wallet
When....* Once

You wrote a title for your next book
At the top of a blank page and the page
Remained blank. *Natural Mother.*
See how your octopus grows

Ghostly white and weak keeping her
Eggs viable. See your whale, her baby
A lifeless appendage. Jettisoned, will she
Feel him, a phantom limb she can't regrow?

There are times dead weight feels better than
Dead loss. On your t.v., another mother weeps
In front of a bank of microphones, pleads with
Police to see the next mother's son as

Someone. Human. Complete. Born into a habitat
Of random violence, my second graders sleep
Through gunfire, somehow sink into blessed sleep
Through siren-slashed nights like these.

SIRENS

i. In Every Story

the songstress is a siren, the siren sings sailors
to watery graves and brave men tie themselves in knots
to avoid her—Ulysses lashed to the mast—
while, home, it is always some Penelope who weaves
and unweaves, reciting and interrupting her story.

What is wrong with this picture?

Hear what first seems her silence, an absence,
then hear her hum as she pulls warp through weft
each day, each night as she undoes the tale she weaves,
the heft of her loyalty thick and complex.
She braids her destiny with his, becomes somehow
only one bright thread in the tapestry, somehow
a grace note in his crashing opus. But listen:
you can hear her if you listen.

ii. So Listen

too much silence in the halls of children. Too many princesses
still manacled, beaten, locked in towers. Too many girls and boys
locked in closets until they hear sirens wail,
and a SWAT team leads them out into sun lit streets.

iii. And Out on the Streets

beyond the white pillared castle built for men who once promised never
to be kings, where walls are now guarded to keep subjects from entering,
a young woman steps up to a microphone and her song to the throng
is a list of lost children and after
words, she shuts her mouth, opens her face and her eyes hold us—
hundreds of thousands held rapt, rooted—awaiting her next lyric.

Four minutes tick by,

the only sounds the whisper
of tears down cheeks and feet
shuffling in the streets.

We lean forward,
toward her, a few chants of *Emma, Emma,*
which drift to sighs as she stands still,
her silence loud as wild surf just before
whipped waves send complacent sailors overboard.

SAVE THE CHILDREN

For Miah; for all the Miahs

i.

Once, having broken another limb, ankle or collar or hip, my brittle-boned, sweet-souled sister, for weeks unable to sleep or pace, taped a portrait of a cherub-faced boy from some starving, far away nation on her refrigerator where she could greet him when she had her tea in the morning. *I ran out of things to buy on HSN at 2 a.m.,* she explained, *so I got "Anhelo" off Save the Children,* and though we both laughed—starving child as impulse buy—she sent her monthly dollars religiously, long past when letters and updates arrived, the child a man by then and who knew where.

ii.

An American sickness, Simon says. As in
Simon says take two steps, backward, you think
reading of another school, the whispered pleas
of fledglings under desks, left unanswered.

iii.

Snakes grow shed regrow skin, we read on the zoo's plaque. *Look at this one,* my grandson gasps, cobra unspooling under his gaze, desultory, behind glass, its yellow diamonded epidermis an argyle sock threaded with gold, shimmers as the cobra shimmies over to stare back at the boy. We wonder what skin it wore before. Ripped, torn—to shed what it's outgrowing, the creature first rubs itself against a rock, rends itself, the raw opening the very place where it will emerge. Squishy soft. Vulnerable for a spell. I read once that to crack its shell, an encased baby bird beats its unfeathered wings against inside walls, beats them almost to exhaustion. To rip itself free, the new butterfly must do the same. *Never, never help,* my mother once told me as I reached to loosen one sticky thread of cocoon. Without the work, no wing becomes strong enough for flight. Tired of the snake, my

grandson weaves in and out among zoo crowds looking for the ancient
tortoise, for a moment beyond my sheltering grasp.

iv.

Tell yourself that any ordeal will strengthen them. Tell yourself that.
Go on, I dare you.

v

Listen. Miah hears his loud, sad music blaring still.
Vacuum at the carwash sets her off, her mother says.
Her hair falls in clumps, her hands can't forget the feel
of her dead friend's blood, that sad music, the way
when she called 9-1-1 for help,
no one came. Why did no one come she asks.
She sits with her parents, swaddled in blankets
despite the Texas heat. She'll never be warm again.
A miracle once already, her mother tells reporters.
Born with a tumor in her abdomen, not supposed to live
past neonate, surgery at three, then thriving.
Dad's cell phone rings and she's shivering again,
mother wondering how many miracles
can one child survive?

WRITE YOUR HOPE FOR THE NEW YEAR

you say, and Dave says *it will be*
marginally better than the last, which,
he admits, *is like saying*

slightly less evil than
Hitler but Corey says *a new moon*
as the new year opens could mean

possibilities, which could go,
given human nature and humans
and nature, either way these days,

and you may call me crazy—
writing letters to the editor when
nobody reads newsprint any more or

for yelling myself hoarse at the walls
behind which my senator hides every
mild or inclement Tuesday. I'll still

knock on doors ranting like Chicken Little
when we all know the sky is ripped
open if not falling and possibly

it's all beyond repair. But listen:
my grandson is teaching himself *Fly*
Eagles Fly on his shiny new trumpet.

Outside, a cold December Wednesday,
I'm standing in a city school yard while
my granddaughter's second grade sings

to shivering, masked parents who want
only the world for their children, proud
smiles hidden by KN95's, and I am here,

recalling how long after her own
illegal but safe abortion, long after
her own menopause, my mother,

newly a grandmother, escorted
terrified girls past a red-faced mob
and into a clean, warm clinic. I'm seeing

my father, at 70, marching in an anti-
nuclear protest for the first time. Call me
crazy for hope: I'm just Sarah Blossom's

Gramma, I'll tell you. I'm just
Bill's third, determined girl. I guess
I'm just Esther's most stubborn child.

HER TOO: Ledor Vador

i.

This, which is and is not for my mother.
This, which is and is not for the island of
Puerto Rico, which is America, which is, yes,

America which is not understood by too many Americans
To be America, paper towels flung at the heads of the bereft
Near drowned, after the hurricane passed through.

This, which is and is not about my mother
About an island crimson with bougainvillea,
Pale blue and breathless after storm, where

Once, long before paper towels were lobbed
Across a room of citizens by not-their- president-
Not-my-president, my mother nearly bled to

Death for no reason she would blame on
Puerto Rico. *Blame America*, she once told me,
And I do.

ii.

At the aquarium in Camden, my small granddaughters are mesmerized
by the dance and drift of tentacled jellyfish, kites floating through a
watery sky blue, through fluid air as if on one perfect day of enough.
Enough wind to raise the kites above the beach. Enough stillness to
keep them there. Enough for me to watch my granddaughters' rapt
believing faces, reflections in the round window of the jellyfish tank,
to guide their small hands into cold waters toward smooth-backed
sting rays, surprisingly lumpy cold limbs of rust-tinged sea stars in the
touching tank. In this, I am become my mother.

iii.

This is about and not about Puerto Rico,
Not about and about my young, pregnant
Mother. This is about my friend Gerard,
Desperate to reach his mother, cell signals
Dead in Puerto Rico, Hurricane Maria
Alive and furious. This is about
Gerard, how he apologized to our collage

Class for his distraction, while we, a group of
Mothers, tried to reassure him, listened to
Dead air on his phone, tore and cut and glued.
Coral of stewed tomatoes, ripped bits of mountain,
A few fish swimming through calm green waters.
I made my landscape under sea, serene: teal, yellow.
No screaming reds of bougainvillea.

iv.

She never learned to swim, my mother,
but she loved to walk along sand.

Transplant to salt-spray and waves,
she spent summer days picking up

beached creatures, running fingers
over smooth shells, bumpy dried skins,

teaching us to name the life by the husk:
razor clam, devil's purse, whelk. Once,

horseshoe crabs washed up, stranded;
on earth long before us, she instructed.

Once a storm blew starfish hoards to shore.
We carried plastic pails to the beach, could not

bail fast enough, next dawn, mourned
the hundreds left to dry.

v.

Then one summer, she disappeared for at least a week from our island. When she returned, she remained far away, pale, stayed out of the sun all day. I picture her now, alone in the shuttered, cool house, how she must have replayed the way the air felt when she deplaned the small prop in Puerto Rico. I picture her hesitation before she entered, on a back street, a clinic where no one spoke English, the only language she had in which to ask for what she needed. Gray, dark, colorless in the memory she finally confessed to us so many years later. Outside, the moist hot air. The unforgettable slashes of red bougainvillea,

I almost died. So many years of silence before we finally heard the confusion—shame/fury—heard of the doctor, stateside, who refused to treat the ceaseless bleeding *because of what I'd done.*

vi.

Blame America, she said.
And I do.

HER STAKE

My daughter has learned to read
the signs
and display them.

She stakes her words, pounds
her stake
into the chill dirt,

into browning grass so
Hate has no home here
is how her lawn

reads in at least three languages.
Where I want
to live she would plant only

next spring's tulips, daffodils, gold
and orange mums
to variegate this autumn.

Maybe she would root and trim
one winterberry shrub,
blood-red nubs staining, transforming,

into the coming winter the white
of snow
blanketing an old inner-ring suburb,

no need to declare, no need
to distinguish
this home from any other.

I DREAM TONI MORRISON WEEDING HER GARDEN

Without gloves, dirt up under her nails,
Hums a church song or some

Sam Cooke, finds slugs and snails and digs them
Deeper into the shale-striped soil. Sweat-faced,

She heaves herself off her knees,
Smile cracking a make-up free face.

What she plants, feeds: lettuces
Carrots, crisp red radishes and beans

Snaking up a green pole like some exotic dancer
Who damn well knows her own worth.

Whatever is inedible still feeds the gardener's
need for scent, for color: blaring

Yellow daffodils, red, orange, pink tea roses.
Everything she lays a glove to flourishes;

She is the creator in Eden by day. By night,
Back at her desk, she tills

The soil of language and novels grow,
Essays bloom. Some she'll prune. Some

She'll feed in scraps to the persistent jays
Outside her bedroom window. A phrase

Here and there she'll mulch into nearly black dirt
aerated by the blind earthworms who are drawn,

As am I, by the almost acrid odor of her
Ink-stained fingers.

VISIBILITY

Let in the light,
the scent of white roses,
faint, but still visible

to the nose as the old year
withers, closes out, dark hours
superseding the bright,

my eyes open, aperature
as extended as possible—
16 dilating drops! I'm not

surprised, the doctor says
when, 30 hours post surgery,
my eyes can't shut out

sparks, halos, shards of lamp-
glow or star-shine.
Nearly the solstice now,

so near the day with as few lit
minutes as this year will offer.
On a sun-warmed bench,

in a well-worn cemetery, I
absorb the peace of the chill
breeze as brown leaves, fallen,

chitter across colonial stones,
speak in their own language.
No need, today, to decode.

OLIVIA AND I LEARN ABOUT THE NATURE OF TIME AND SPACE

Not the shortest day, Olivia corrects,
time is all the same, the days,
I mean. She's reaching for words

to encapsulate what yogis and physicists,
even visionaries can't articulate,
but she doesn't know that yet,

seven years old, maybe eight, a so-large block
of her school life to date spent in a square box
trying to learn science via Zoom

in this season of plague. What must she feel, Olivia,
ten months away from playmates, such dark times,
everything askew? Cold solstice and I learn

Jupiter and Saturn align as light wanes, *one great*
conjunction of the two largest planets in our known system
combining their brightness over a tired city.

Just look south and west, Corina instructs
as I sit on my yoga mat what we call hours later.
There will be such brightness, and is this

irony or blessing on a day when most of the hours
all days contain will be spent in darkness
before the world tilts back. In second grade,

I learned only of time's forward motion, learned
never to hold still in the now as now, nearing seventy,
I hold still, this Great Conjunction glimmering.

Liz Abrams-Morley's collections include *Beholder*, 2018, *Inventory*, 2014 and *Necessary Turns*, published by Word Poetry in 2010 and which won an Eric Hoffer Award for Excellence in Small Press Publishing that year. In 2020 she was named the Passager Poet of the year in *Passager Journal*'s annual contest. Liz's poems and short stories have been published in a variety of nationally distributed anthologies, journals and ezines, and have been read on NPR.

She has collaborated with visual artists on artist books and art installations, and co-authored a textbook on the use of poetry and book arts to be used in the K-12 classroom. In recent years, Abrams-Morley has been sometimes working as a collage artist. In 2023, she collaborated with her sister, the visual artist Pam Abrams-Warnick on a visual art piece based on Liz's poem, "October's End: Eve Returns to the Garden," which was admitted into a juried show that year.

A semi-retired faculty member in the Rosemont College MFA program, Liz is co-founder of Around the Block Writers' Collaborative. A poet, professor, gramma and activist, Liz wades knee deep in the flow of everyday life from which she draws inspiration and, occasionally, exasperation.

Please visit her on the web at *www.lizabramsmorley.com*